MY SPARKLING BOOK OF

FRUIT

Published by :

DREAMLAND PUBLICATIONS

J-128, KIRTI NAGAR, NEW DELHI-110 015 (INDIA)
PHONE : 011- 2510 6050, FAX : 011- 2543 8283
E-mail : dreamland@vsnl.com
www.dreamlandpublications.com

APPLE

MANGO

PEAR

2

GUAVA

STRAWBERRY

BANANA

PAPAYA

PINEAPPLE

3

LIME

TANGERINES
OR MANDARINS

GRAPEFRUIT

CARAMBOLA
STAR FRUIT

ORANGE

4

CITRON

TAMARILLO

LOQUAT

PRICKLY PEAR

KIWI

PASSION FRUIT

MELON

KIWANO

WATERMELON

6

JUJUBE

KUMQUAT

AVOCADO

7

SAPODILLA (CHICKOO)

LOGANBERRY

CHERIMOYA

RAMBUTAN

SOURSOP

8

MEDLAR

OLIVE

CUSTARD APPLE

NECTARINE

PEACH

APRICOT

9

PLUM

RED CURRANT

GOOSEBERRY

CHERRY

BLUEBERRY

GRAPES

10

RASPBERRY

MULBERRY

BLACKBERRY

11

QUINCE

CACAO

DRAGON FRUIT

POMEGRANATE

PHYSALIS

MANGOSTEEN

BABACOS

CURUBA

13

SALAK / SNAKE FRUIT

FEIJOA

PEPINO

DURIAN

POMELO

EMBLIC

CITRON

PERSIMMON

FIG

DATE

COCONUT

16